MW01000214

Can Lightning Strike the Same Place Twice?

And Other Questions about Earth, Weather, and the Environment

JOANNE MATTERN

ILLUSTRATIONS BY COLIN W. THOMPSON

LERNER PUBLICATIONS COMPANY

Minneapolis

Contents

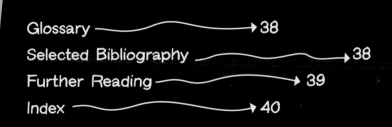

Introduction

Perhaps you've heard these common sayings or beliefs about Earth, weather, and the environment:

Lightning can't strike the same place twice! Earth is running out of landfill space!

But are these sayings true? Is there any science behind the stories? Come along with us as we explore these old beliefs and more. Find out whether the stories and sayings you hear every day are **FACT OR FICTION!**

Does a Ring Around the Moon Really Mean Rain or Snow Is on the Way?

YES, it often means that wet weather is coming. To understand why, you need to know what causes the ring.

The ring you sometimes see around the moon is not a real ring, like the ones around the planet Saturn. It is caused by moonlight shining on a type of cloud called cirrostratus. Cirrostratus clouds form very high in the atmosphere. These clouds contain ice crystals. As rays of light from the moon pass through the crystals, the rays bend at a sharp angle. From Earth, it looks as if there is a ring around the moon.

So why does a ring around the moon signal that bad weather may be coming? Because cirrostratus clouds are often followed by storm clouds.

The moon has a ring around it in the photo above because of the cirrostratus clouds (background image) in the night sky.

Once those big, heavy storm clouds arrive, the ring will disappear. In fact, you may not be able to see the moon at all. But if you're outside, you will soon get wet!

Can Lightning Strike the Same Place Twice?

YES, IT CAN! Many places have been hit by lightning more than once. Tall buildings and trees are often targets of lightning bolts. That's because they are closer to the storm clouds than objects that are nearer to the ground, such as your family's car. Some famous places are real lightning magnets. The Empire State Building in New York City is one example. Lightning hits it about twenty-five times a year!

Lightning strikes the Empire State Building in New York City many times each year.

The lightning in this photo is easy to see against the large, dark thunderclouds. You can see rain falling from the clouds as well.

Lightning comes from a thundercloud with a very strong electrical charge. Why does it strike? To understand why, it helps to know that everything is made of tiny atoms—even you! And atoms have two parts that carry electrical charges. They're called electrons and protons. Electrons have a negative charge. Protons have a positive charge. During a storm, the atoms in a thundercloud sometimes have many more electrons than protons. The cloud builds up a big negative charge. And electrons naturally flow from places with negative charges to places with positive charges. This means that the electrons in the cloud will try to move to a place with a positive charge—such as the ground. When the electrons get close to an object on the ground, the object responds to the strong electrical field in the air. It sends out electrical energy of its own. A surge of energy rushes back to the cloud. Bam! A lightning bolt flashes against the sky.

This model shows electrons circling around the nucleus of an atom.

Tall objects—such as skyscrapers, trees, or radio towers—create an easy path for the electrons to travel as they move from the storm cloud to the ground. That's why they can get hit again and again.

Is It True That You Can Dig a Hole from One Side of Earth to the Other?

Have you ever wanted to dig a hole in your backyard? We're talking about a really BIG hole—one that could reach all the way to the other side of Earth. This may sound like a fun idea, but you probably wouldn't get very far before you gave up. And you wouldn't be able to dig to the other side of Earth anyway. THIS IS ONE BELIEF THAT IS TOTALLY FALSE.

This diagram of Earth shows the three different layers that make up our planet.

Crust

Mantle

Core

The surface of Earth is made up of rocks and dirt. But a lot more is going on inside our planet than you can see from the surface. Earth has three different layers. The outer layer— all those rocks and dirt—is called the crust. The crust is about 18 feet (5.5 meters) deep in most places. But it is much thinner under the ocean and much thicker in the mountains.

The second layer is the mantle. The mantle extends about 1,800 miles (2,897 km) beneath the crust. This layer is made of thick, hot, semisolid rock. Lots of minerals, such as iron, are in this layer too. This layer is so hot and thick that it would be impossible to dig through with a shovel.

The third and deepest layer of Earth is the core. The core is even hotter and thicker than the mantle. The core has two parts. The outer part is a layer of hot liquid that is 1,360°F (738°C). Inside that is a 775-mile-thick (1,247 km) solid inner core.

Now think of all the thousands of miles and all the red-hot material you would have to dig through to reach the other side of Earth. Do you see why digging through our planet is impossible?

Is It Safe to Go Outside While the Eye of a Hurricane Is Passing over Your Home?

THE ANSWER TO THIS ONE IS ABSOLUTELY NOT! To understand why, let's look at how a hurricane works.

Hurricanes can cause a lot of damage when they come ashore.

You can see the clouds spinning around the eye of Hurricane Katrina, which hit the Gulf Coast of the United States in 2005.

A hurricane is a powerful storm that forms in the southern Atlantic Ocean, the Caribbean Sea, the Gulf of Mexico, or the eastern Pacific Ocean. All of these places have very warm water, which is a key ingredient for cooking up a hurricane. These storms gather energy as water evaporates from the surface of a warm ocean. If conditions are right, the warm, moist air rises in a column and starts to spin around an area of low pressure. This spinning can create a large storm with strong winds of more than 74 miles (119 km) per hour. Because hurricanes are large storms, they usually last for several days.

During a hurricane, clouds spin around the center, or eye, of the storm. The clouds around the eye are called the eyewall. These clouds often produce intense thunder and lightning. However, the eye of the storm is very calm. It's not stormy at all.

When the eye of the hurricane passes over a place, the winds and rain often stop. Things get quiet and calm. Many people think the storm is over. They may go outside to check out any storm damage. Then they can get a nasty surprise. As the eye passes, the other side of the hurricane unleashes its wind and rain. Often the wind and rain are even more powerful on this side of the storm. So it's always best to remain inside and stay safe until you hear that the storm is really over.

Hurricane Names

In 1953, the U.S. Weather Bureau began giving hurricanes women's names. In 1979, the Weather Bureau started to use men's names too. Has *your* name ever been used for a hurricane? Visit this website to find out: http://www.nhc .noaa.gov/aboutnames.shtml.

Can People Be Swallowed Up by a Crack in the Earth during an Earthquake?

Maybe you've seen this in a disaster movie: An earthquake strikes, and huge cracks open in the ground. They swallow houses, cars, and people. Could this happen in real life? **NOT A CHANCE.**

Earthquakes happen because the surface of Earth is always in motion. Earth's crust is divided into giant plates. These plates move because liquid rock deep inside Earth is always moving. Sometimes the plates rub against one another. Or one plate will sink underneath another one. Pressure builds up at these spots. When the pressure becomes too strong, the plates move violently. Sometimes a plate even breaks. That's when an earthquake occurs.

It's true that earthquakes are very powerful. It's also true that they can cause tremendous damage. They may even create a hole in the ground. A person could fall into such a hole and be injured—or possibly killed. But the hole just wouldn't be large enough to hold crowds of people, homes, or cars and trucks.

The Richter Scale

Earthquakes are measured by the Richter scale. This scale measures the total amount of force released during an earthquake. Anything over 7.0 on the scale is a major earthquake. The most powerful earthquake to hit the United States occurred in Prince William Sound on March 27, 1964. This monster earthquake measured 9.2 on the Richter scale. It caused tremendous damage to the city of Anchorage, Alaska, which was only 75 miles (120 km) from the center of the quake.

Should You Open Windows in a House to Prevent Damage during a Tornado?

NO! IT IS NOT A GOOD IDEA TO OPEN WINDOWS. If a tornado is on the way, leave the windows alone. Instead, you should focus on finding shelter. Fast! A good place to take shelter is a basement or an inside room away from windows.

Tornado Alley

Half the tornadoes that hit the United States blow through Tornado Alley. What's that? It's a nickname for an area that stretches across the center of the country. Tornado Alley has no specific boundaries, but some states that lie within it include Texas, Oklahoma, Kansas, and Nebraska.

This tornado touched down in South Dakota, which is in Tornado Alley.

A tornado's winds are very powerful. A really strong tornado's winds can blow more than 300 miles (485 km) per hour! That makes tornadoes one of the most violent forces on Earth. The winds can easily rip off siding or break the windows on a house. They can even blow the roof off. Once the roof is gone, the walls will fall in and the house will collapse. That's why taking shelter in a safe place is so important.

People used to think that opening windows in a house during a tornado would prevent the house from exploding. Why would a house explode during a tornado? Scientists once thought that tornadoes forced a lot of air inside the house. After a short time, the air pressure inside the house would be greater than the air pressure outside. This would push out the walls of the house. Today scientists know that the idea of exploding houses isn't true. The biggest danger from tornadoes doesn't come from air pressure. It comes from wind.

Are Forest Fires Really Always Bad?

NOPE. Forest fires seem like a terrible thing, and many times they are. Fires can destroy acres of forest and badly damage the habitats of animals and plants. If a fire gets out of control, it can also threaten people and their property. But believe it or not, forest fires can **actually be a good thing!** In fact, they're necessary to keep forests healthy and diverse.

This forest has new growth after a fire.

Forest fires that start naturally are usually caused by lightning. Lightning strikes are a normal part of nature. The fires they cause are also a normal and necessary part of the life cycle of the forest. These fires are helpful because they clear out thick undergrowth. They thin out trees and let in more light. New plants have more room to grow. Some plants actually rely on forest fires to reproduce. The cones of the jack pine will not open except in the intense heat of a fire. Fires can cause the rebirth of a forest.

The National Park Service uses controlled fires to clear out forests and promote the growth of new plants. These fires are set and carefully managed so they don't get out of control.

Of course, fires can be terribly dangerous. Too many forest fires are set by people who were careless with matches or campfires. It's always best to let nature do its own housekeeping and let the forests take care of themselves!

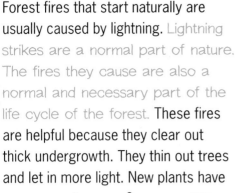

A jack pine tree branch

Did You Know?

Evergreen trees, such as pine trees, burn five to ten times faster than deciduous trees, which lose their leaves every year. That's because the bark and needles of evergreen trees are filled with sap, which catches fire easily.

Is It True That No Two Snowflakes Are Alike?

Have you always heard that no two snowflakes are alike? **SCIENTISTS THINK THE SAYING IS PROBABLY TRUE.** But they can't be sure.

Snowflakes are made up of tiny ice crystals. The crystals form in the clouds. A snowflake can contain several hundred crystals. The crystals can be arranged in a huge number of different patterns. This means the odds are excellent that they will never be arranged the same way twice. That's why people have always believed that no two snowflakes are alike.

However, not *all* snowflakes are made up of a large number of crystals. Some contain only a few different crystals. Since these snowflakes have fewer crystals, there is a better chance that the crystals may be arranged in the same way. That would mean that there just might be two snowflakes that are alike.

Scientists will never be able to prove whether two snowflakes are alike by looking at them. There are just too many snowflakes to check them all! In any given year, about 1 quadrillion cubic feet (28 trillion cubic m) of snow falls on our planet. (That's right—1 *quadrillion* cubic feet!) So how could a scientist figure out the chances of two snowflakes being exactly the same? The scientist could use math to figure out the odds. And the math suggests that two snowflakes could probably be exactly alike—but the possibility is very, very small.

Try This!

If you live in a cold climate, here's a fun activity you can try the next time it snows. First, find a black sheet of construction paper. Then see if you can find a magnifying glass. (The activity will work without the magnifying glass, but it will be easier if you have one on hand.)

Now take the paper and the magnifying glass outside. Use the paper to catch as many snowflakes as you can. The flakes should show up very well against the black background.

Next, examine the flakes closely and see how many differences you spot among them. (This is where the magnifying glass will come in handy.) Do you see crystals with starfish shapes? Arrowheads? Diamonds?

From this activity, it should be easy to see that snowflakes can be truly unique!

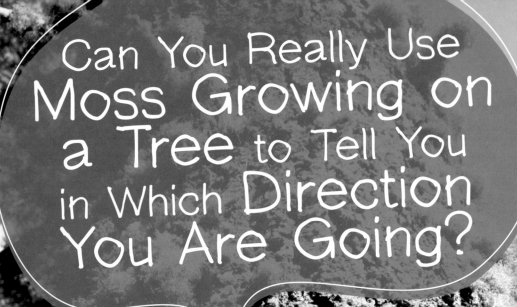

Can You Really Use Moss Growing on a Tree to Tell You in Which Direction You Are Going?

Maybe this question occurred to you while you were reading an adventure story or watching a movie. The hero escapes from the bad guys and gets lost in the woods. He or she looks at the bottom of a tree trunk and announces that moss is growing there. The hero says the mossy side of the tree has to be the northern side. Once the hero knows which direction is north, it's easier for him or her to find the way to safety. Could this happen in real life? **THE ANSWER IS PROBABLY YES—IF YOU LIVE IN THE NORTHERN HEMISPHERE (NORTH OF THE EQUATOR).**

Moss is a kind of plant that grows where it's damp and cool. Forests are usually damp and cool because of all the shade from trees. And the northern side of a tree is usually coolest in the Northern Hemisphere. That's because the sun doesn't shine on that side as much. So that's where moss will usually thrive.

Moss can grow on any side of a tree in a very shady forest like this one.

However, in a very thick forest, moss may grow in places other than the north side of a tree. Why? Because all those trees give so much shade that the sun can't reach the south, east, or west sides either. So in an extremely woodsy area, the moss trick may not work as well.

This tree has moss growing on one of its sides.

Is It True That Water Drains in a Different Direction in Each Hemisphere?

NO! Many people believe the force of Earth's rotation on its axis makes water drain in a counterclockwise direction in the Northern Hemisphere and a clockwise direction in the Southern Hemisphere. But it's not true. The force that makes the water drain in one direction in your sink or toilet has to do with the plumbing in your home. It depends on how the sink or toilet fills in the first place.

Under certain weather conditions, the rotation of Earth does make winds spin counterclockwise in the Northern Hemisphere and clockwise in the Southern Hemisphere. **The easiest way to see this is to look at a photo of a hurricane. You can see that the winds spin around a center of low air pressure. And the direction of the winds depends on whether the storm is north or south of the equator.**

The connection between the way the winds churn and the rotation of Earth is called the Coriolis effect.

However, the Coriolis effect doesn't work on bathtub or sink drains because the rotation of Earth is very slow. **It rotates only once a day. The water in your sink makes a rotation in just a few seconds. The rotation of Earth just isn't a strong enough force to affect water swirling down your drain.**

Australia

The winds in this Southern Hemisphere hurricane spin clockwise.

Can You Tell How Far Away a Storm Is by Counting the Seconds Between a Flash of Lightning and a Roll of Thunder?

YES, you can get a rough idea of how far away a thunderstorm is by counting the seconds between lightning flashes and thunder rumbles.

Here's how to do it: As soon as you see lightning, start counting the seconds. Stop when you hear the thunder. Then divide the number of seconds you counted by five. The answer is the number of miles between you and the storm. The lower the number, the closer the storm. If the lightning and thunder occur almost at the same time, the storm is right overhead.

The reason this formula works is that light moves faster than sound. Thunder and lightning actually happen at the same time. But we see the light before we hear the thunder. Light travels so fast that we see it right away. However, it takes a few seconds for the sound of thunder to reach us.

It is never safe to be outside during a thunderstorm. Even if the lightning struck several miles away, an electrical charge could be building very close to you. So be sure to do your storm counting from inside the house!

These thunderclouds are illuminated by flashes of lightning over Tucson, Arizona.

Did You Know?

Thunderstorms are most likely to occur in the spring and summer, but they can also happen during snowstorms!

Is It True That the Great Wall of China Is the Only Human-Made Object You Can See from Space?

NOPE. The idea that you can see the Great Wall from space has been around since 1938. That's when the claim appeared in *Richard Halliburton's Second Book of Marvels*. In the book, Halliburton said that the Great Wall was the only human-made object that could be seen from the moon. Since no one set foot on the moon until 1969, it's not clear where Halliburton got the evidence for this statement. But people believed him for many years.

In this satellite image of Earth, the red arrows point to the Great Wall of China.

Great Indeed!

The Great Wall was built more than two thousand years ago. Its purpose was to keep invading armies out of China. The wall didn't work too well for keeping out invaders. But it's still a pretty impressive sight! The wall is about 3,700 miles (6,000 km) long.

Astronaut Alan Bean flew to the moon in 1969. He was aboard *Apollo 12*. He said the only things he could see from the moon were patches of color showing clouds, oceans, and deserts. He could not see any human-made objects. Other astronauts who went to the moon have also said no human-made objects were visible from that far away.

However, if you think of space as beginning about 100 miles (160 km) from Earth's surface, then the Great Wall *can* be seen from space. The space shuttle travels between 160 and 350 miles (257 and 563 km) above Earth. And shuttle astronauts have been able to see the Great Wall from that distance. But they have also been able to see other human structures, including highways, bridges, dams, and airports. So while it's true that you can see the Great Wall from a low Earth orbit, it's also true that you can see plenty of other objects.

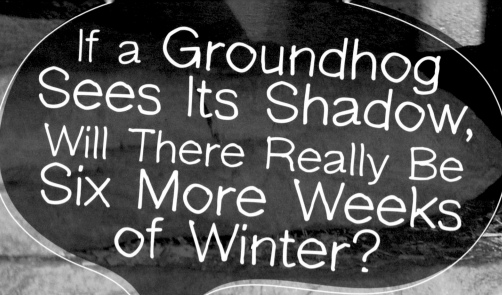

If a Groundhog Sees Its Shadow, Will There Really Be Six More Weeks of Winter?

NO! According to one of the United States' oldest winter traditions, the groundhog wakes up from hibernation on Groundhog Day, which falls on February 2. If it's a sunny day and the groundhog sees its shadow, it will go back to its burrow and hibernate for another six weeks. This means another six weeks of winter. But if it's cloudy and the groundhog can't see its shadow, the groundhog will stay out of its burrow. And spring will arrive earlier.

The truth is that the groundhog has nothing to do with whether winter weather will end early or last a long time. And regardless of the weather, spring always comes on or around March 21, no matter what the groundhog sees!

Badger

Buds begin to open on a branch in early spring.

The idea that a groundhog could predict the length of the winter goes back to the 1700s. That's when large numbers of German immigrants began arriving in the United States. Back in Germany, the behavior of an animal called the badger had been thought of as a good weather predictor. The groundhog looks like the badger, and both of these animals hibernate underground through the winter. But the groundhog is a lot more common in the United States than the badger. So the Germans began to use the groundhog to guess whether winter would be long or short.

Is It True That Earth Is Running Out of Landfill Space?

NO. There is plenty of empty land in the United States for new landfills for burying trash. But getting rid of garbage is a big problem. Many landfills are full or almost full, especially those in areas with large populations. It is not unusual for cities to truck their garbage to landfills hundreds of miles away.

Most people will fight any effort to build a landfill in their neighborhood. They don't want a bunch of smelly garbage nearby. Also, it takes a lot of planning to build a landfill. Engineers and other scientists have to pick a good site. They need to make sure the site isn't near any water sources.

That's because garbage from a landfill can run into the water and pollute it.

One way to help solve the trash disposal problem is for all of us to produce less garbage in the first place. And we're making progress! Americans recycle about a third of their trash. That's a good thing—because they produce about 4 pounds (2 kilograms) of garbage per day per person. That adds up to 600,000 tons (544,000 metric tons) of garbage every day, or 210 million tons (190 million metric tons) every year.

Did You Know?

People used to toss their trash into a hole or dump it in a field. They left it there to rot. It attracted rats, flies, and other pests that spread disease. Rain washed dirt and poisons into the water supply. It was a smelly, unhealthful way to get rid of trash. In 1937, the first sanitary landfill in the United States opened in Fresno, California. Sanitary landfills are lined with clay or plastic to keep the garbage from polluting the ground and water sources.

Does Earth's Distance from the Sun Really Cause the Seasons?

NOPE. Many people think summer occurs when Earth is closer to the sun and winter occurs when Earth is farther away from it. And that seems to make sense, doesn't it? Wouldn't you guess that Earth would warm up when it got near the sun and cool down as it moved away? But that's not how it works. In fact, Earth is closest to the sun in January, when it is winter in North America. And it's farthest away from the sun in July, when many of us are wearing shorts and sandals!

The seasons occur because Earth tilts on its axis as it revolves around the sun. As a result of this tilt, the sun shines directly on only part of Earth at a time. The sun shines directly over the Northern Hemisphere around June 21, when summer begins in that part of the world. It shines directly over the Southern Hemisphere around December 21. That's when summer begins in countries such as Australia and Argentina.

So Earth's movement does influence the seasons. However, Earth's distance from the sun has nothing to do with it. Instead, it's Earth's slight tilt that gives us winter, spring, summer, and fall.

This illustration shows how Earth is tilted on its axis. This means that the Northern Hemisphere is tilted toward the sun part of the year, and the Southern Hemisphere is tilted toward the sun the rest of the year.

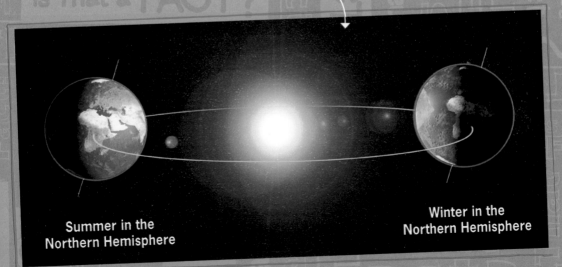

Summer in the
Northern Hemisphere

Winter in the
Northern Hemisphere

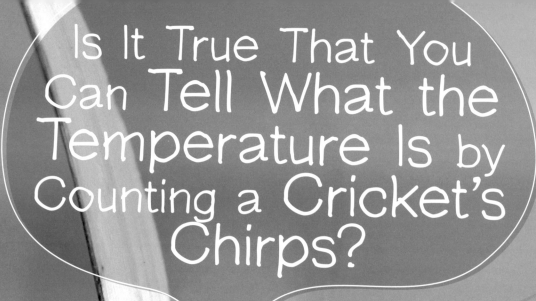

Is It True That You Can Tell What the Temperature Is by Counting a Cricket's Chirps?

Did you guess no? This bit of weather folklore sounds as if it should be false. But believe it or not, **IT IS ACTUALLY TRUE!** A cricket's chirps won't give you the exact temperature. But they *can* give you a very good idea of how hot or cold it is.

Crickets chirp by rubbing their wings together. Usually males do the chirping. The insect rubs a sharp edge on one wing against some bumps on the other wing to make the chirping sound. Males usually chirp to attract the attention of a female. They also chirp when they are fighting with another male or to sound an alert if danger is near.

To use a cricket's chirp to tell the temperature, you have to count the number of chirps in 15 seconds. Then add 39 to the total. The answer will be the temperature in degrees Fahrenheit. You can also count the chirps in 13 seconds and then add 40 to the total. These formulas are usually accurate to within 1 degree of the actual temperature.

This weather trick works because crickets are cold-blooded. That means their body temperature is the same as the air around them. When a cricket gets cold, its body temperature drops and it becomes less active. A cold cricket chirps less often than a warm cricket. So the more the insect chirps, the higher the temperature.

Is It True That All Deserts Are Hot?

NO! When you think of a desert, you probably think of a sandy place where the sun beats down and the air is superhot. Some deserts are like that. But not every desert is hot. Several are actually freezing cold.

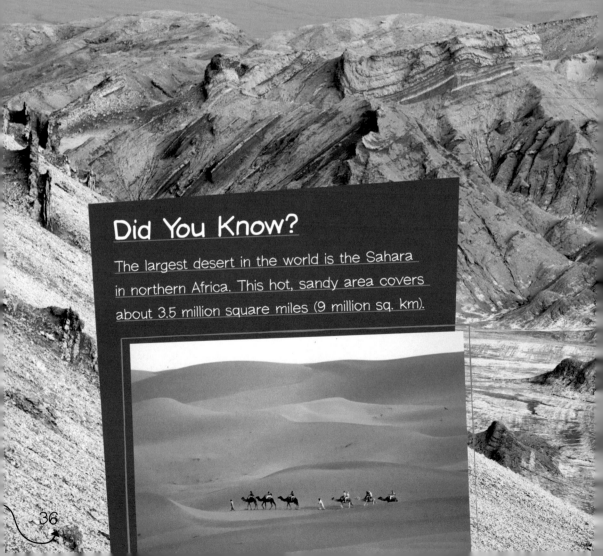

Did You Know?

The largest desert in the world is the Sahara in northern Africa. This hot, sandy area covers about 3.5 million square miles (9 million sq. km).

The key factor that makes a place a desert is not temperature. It is dryness. A desert receives less than 19 inches (48 centimeter) of rain each year.

One of the driest deserts in the world is the Atacama Desert in northern Chile. This desert receives less than 0.5 inch (1.3 cm) of rain each year. Winters are cool there. The temperature can be as low as 32°F (0°C). In the summer, it may rise as high as 77°F (25°C). That's a lot cooler than the Mojave Desert in the western United States, where the temperature can reach a scorching 120°F (49°C).

Even deserts that are very hot during the day can cool down quickly at night. The air in a desert is so dry that it does not hold a lot of heat. So as soon as the sun goes down, the heat escapes into the atmosphere. That leaves the desert dry and cold until the sun comes up again to warm things up.

ATACAMA
Desert

GLOSSARY

air pressure: the density or weight of the air

atmosphere: the mixture of gases that surrounds a planet

atom: the tiniest part of a substance that has all of that substance's qualities

axis: an imaginary line through the middle of an object, around which that object spins

cirrostratus: a high, thin cloud that contains ice crystals

cold-blooded: having a body temperature that changes according to the temperature of the surroundings

core: the very hot inner part of Earth

Coriolis effect: the movement of objects, including clouds, in a clockwise or counterclockwise direction because of the rotation of Earth

crust: the hard outer layer of Earth

crystal: something that forms a pattern of many flat surfaces when it becomes solid, such as a snowflake or salt

earthquake: a violent movement in Earth's crust

electron: a tiny particle in an atom that carries a negative charge

hemisphere: half of a sphere or round object, such as Earth

hurricane: a violent storm with high winds and heavy rain

landfill: an area where garbage is buried

mantle: the part of Earth between the crust and the core

pollute: to make dirty or impure

proton: a tiny particle in an atom that carries a positive charge

Richter scale: a scale that measures the strength of an earthquake by the amount of energy released

tornado: a violent windstorm with a funnel-shaped cloud

SELECTED BIBLIOGRAPHY

Burt, Christopher G. *Extreme Weather.* New York: W. W. Norton and Company, 2004.

EarthSky Communications. "Earth & Sky Science Podcasts." Earth and Sky.org. 2009. http://www.earthsky.org (June 8, 2009).

How Stuff Works. "How Lightning Works." How Stuff Works.com. 2009. http://www.howstuffworks.com/lightning.htm. (June 8, 2009).

McVey, Vicki. *The Sierra Club Book of Weather Wisdom.* San Francisco: Sierra Club Books, 1991.

Murch, Barbara. *Geology: A Self-Teaching Guide.* New York: Wiley, 2001.

"Myths and Misconceptions about Tornadoes." The Tornado Project Online. 1999. http://www.tornadoproject.com/myths/myths.htm (June 8, 2009).

Regents of the University of California. "The Desert Biome." University of California Museum of Paleontology. N.d. http://www.ucmp.berkeley.edu/exhibits/biomes/deserts.php (June 8, 2009).

Robinson, Andrew. *Earth Shock: Hurricanes, Volcanoes, Earthquakes, Tornadoes, and Other Forces of Nature.* London: Thames and Hudson, 2002.

"Snowflakes: No Two Alike?"
Snowcrystal.com. 1999. http://www.its
.caltech.edu/~atomic/snowcrystals/
alike/alike.htm (June 8, 2009).

"Urban Legends Reference Page: Great
Wall from Space." Snopes.com. 2007.
http://www.snopes.com/science/
greatwall.asp (June 8, 2009).

U.S. Geological Survey. "Inside the Earth."
USGS. 1999. http://pubs.usgs.gov/gip/
dynamic/inside.html (June 8, 2009).

"WeatherSavvy—Lightning."
WeatherSavvy.com. N.d. http://
weathersavvy.com/Lightning.html
(June 8, 2009).

"A Whole Lotta Shakin' Goin' On." State of
California Department of Conservation.
2007. http://www.conservation.ca.gov/
index/Earthquakes/Pages/
qh_earthquakes.aspx (June 8, 2009).

FURTHER READING

Berger, Melvin, and Gilda Berger.
*Hurricanes Have Eyes but Can't See: And
Other Amazing Facts about Wild Weather.*
New York: Scholastic, 2003. You'll enjoy
this delightful collection of fun facts and
surprising information about storms and
other weather conditions.

Challoner, Jack. *Hurricane and Tornado.*
New York: DK Publishing, 2004. In this
fascinating book, you'll find a detailed
look at how hurricanes and tornadoes
form, the damage they can do, and how
people study them.

FEMA for Kids
http://www.fema.gov/kids
Check out this website, sponsored by the
Federal Emergency Management Agency,
for facts and safety tips about weather
conditions and natural disasters.

Groundhog Day: Is It Spring Yet?
http://wilstar.com/holidays/grndhog
.htm
Discover the truth behind Groundhog
Day at this entertaining site.

Only You Can Prevent Wildfires
http://www.smokeybear.com/natural
.asp
Smokey the Bear provides information
about forest fires at this interesting
website.

Packard, Mary. *Mythbusters: Don't Try
This At Home!* San Francisco: Jossey-
Bass, 2006. Come along with Adam
Savage and Jamie Hyneman—stars of
the popular Discovery Channel show
Mythbusters—as they put fifteen beliefs
about the natural world, animals, and
more to the test.

Vogt, Gregory. *Is There Life on Other
Planets?: And Other Questions about
Space.* Minneapolis: Lerner Publications Company, 2010. Find out whether
seventeen common sayings and beliefs
about space are really true.

What's the Weather?
http://www.bbg.org/gar2/topics/
essays/2006fa_weather.html
This fun website of the Brooklyn Botanic
Garden explains some natural ways to
predict the weather.

Woods, Michael, and Mary B. Woods.
Earthquakes. Minneapolis: Lerner
Publications Company, 2007. This book
describes how and why earthquakes
occur and the damage they can do.

———. *Hurricanes.* Minneapolis: Lerner
Publications Company, 2007. This book
provides a close-up look at hurricanes.

INDEX

ACKNOWLEDGMENTS
The images in this book are used with the permission of: © Jerry Horn/Dreamstime.com, pp. 1, 25; © iStockphoto.com/Jan Rysavy, pp. 2 (top), 4; NOAA's National Weather Service (NWS) Collection, pp. 2 (bottom), 18–19 (snowflakes); © Tim Gainey/Gap Photo/Visuals Unlimited, Inc., pp. 3, 34; © iStockphoto.com/Charles Schug, p. 5 (background); © George Frey/Getty Images, p. 5; © Mark Atkins/Dreamstime.com, pp. 6–7; © Nic Fulton/Reuters/CORBIS, p. 6; © John Giustina/Iconica/Getty Images, p. 7 (top); © Leigh Prather/Dreamstime.com, p. 7 (bottom); © Philip and Karen Smith/Photographer's Choice RF/Getty Images, pp. 8–9; © Gary Hincks/Photo Researchers, Inc., p. 9; © Mark Lewis/Photographer's Choice/Getty Images, pp. 10–11; © Mark Wilson/Getty Images, p. 10; NASA, p. 11; © Liu Jin/AFP/Getty Images, pp. 12–13; © Rob Stegmann/Dreamstime.com, p. 14; © Chris White/Dreamstime.com, p. 15 (top); © Steve Pope/Getty Images, p. 15 (bottom); © Mark Thiessen/National Geographic/Getty Images, pp. 16–17; © Inga Spence/Visuals Unlimited, Inc., p. 16; © Jason Johnson, p. 17; © Phil Schermeister/National Geographic/Getty Images, p. 18; © TimurD-Fotolia.com, p. 19 (magnifying glass); © Chris Rodenberg/Dreamstime.com, p. 20; © Andrei Calangiu/Dreamstime.com, p. 21 (top); © Dalibor Kantor/Dreamstime.com, p. 21 (bottom); © Kingjon/Dreamstime.com, p. 22; © NOAA/Getty Images, p. 23; © Photodisc/Getty Images, p. 24; © Pacific Stock/SuperStock, pp. 26–27; Image Science and Analysis Laboratory, NASA-Johnson Space Center, p. 26; © Archie Carpenter/Getty Images, p. 28; © Krzysztof Korolonek/Dreamstime.com, p. 29 (left); © Twildlife/Dreamstime.com, p. 29 (right); © Jeri Gleiter/Taxi/Getty Images, pp. 30–31; © iStockphoto.com/Tryfonov Ievgenii, p. 32; © Anna Rogal/Dreamstime.com, p. 33 (top); © Karsten Schneider/Photo Researchers, Inc., p. 33 (bottom); © Amy Nicolai/Dreamstime.com, p. 35 (left); © Christina Ferrin/Dreamstime.com, p. 35 (right); © Gavin Hellier/Robert Harding World Imagery/Getty Images, pp. 36–37; © Mypix/Dreamstime.com, p. 36.

Front Cover: © Photodisc/Getty Images.

Lerner Publications Company
A division of Lerner Publishing Group, Inc.
241 First Avenue North
Minneapolis, MN 55401 U.S.A.

Website address: www.lernerbooks.com

Library of Congress Cataloging-in-Publication Data

Mattern, Joanne, 1963–
    Can lightning strike the same place twice? : and other questions about Earth, weather, and the environment / by Joanne Mattern.
        p.   cm. — (Is that a fact?)
    Includes bibliographical references and index.
    ISBN 978–0–8225–9081–1 (lib. bdg. : alk. paper)
    1. Science—Miscellanea— Juvenile literature. I. Title.
Q163.M45 2010
550—dc22   2009020588

Manufactured in the United States of America
1 – JR – 12/15/09